LANDSCAPE ARCHITECTURE:
WATER FEATURES

ROCKPORT

LANDSCAPE ARCHITECTURE:
WATER FEATURES

GLOUCESTER MASSACHUSETTS

ROCKPORT
PUBLISHERS

First published in the United States of America by
Rockport Publishers, a member of
Quayside Publishing Group
33 Commercial Street
Gloucester, MA 01930-0589
Telephone: (978) 282-9590
Fax: (978) 283-2742
www.rockpub.com

ISBN-13: 978-1-59253-273-5
ISBN-10: 1-59253-273-X

Editor:
Alejandro Bahamón

Research:
Àlex Campello

Editorial coordination:
Catherine Collin

Art Director:
Mireia Casanovas Soley

Graphic Design and Layout:
Oriol Serra Juncosa

Editorial project:
2006 © LOFT Publications
Via Laietana 32, 4th Of. 92.
08003 Barcelona, Spain
Tel.: +34 932 688 088
Fax: +34 932 687 073
loft@loftpublications.com
www.loftpublications.com

Printed in China

Introduction

Over the years different methods have been used to introduce water into garden design. Water played a vital role in the Arabian garden and great subtlety was required to create sophisticated compositions due to the scarcity of this precious liquid. In the Italian Renaissance, water elements were used in abundance, where the uneven lie of the land could result in dynamic features such as waterfalls, fountains, or ponds, which facilitated the creation of focal points. During the French baroque period the same effects were created in totally flat landscapes, which called for the development of hydraulic systems and technology applicable to garden design. On the other hand, the model of the romantic English garden allowed natural forms to be incorporated in the garden design. Today the public feels the need to enhance and be a part of the landscape. The fountains, water ways, and ponds continue to have a decorative and sculptural character, but they are also for the enjoyment of everyone. Contemporary design searches for strategies which incorporate into the town's fabric natural forms of water, such as rivers, lakes, and waterfronts. The following pages present the latest contributions by landscapers from all over the world in the design of water elements in public spaces.

Parks

Parks

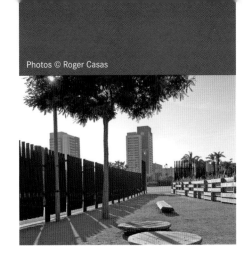

Diagonal Mar Park | **EMBT Arquitectes Associates**

Barcelona, Spain, 2002   Although this park is about the same size as other large gardens in Barcelona, its design and location make it appear larger. The park is situated at the end of Diagonal Avenue, a large urban axis which cuts across the city and finishes up on the waterfront. The connection with this street on the one hand and with the beach on the other facilitates the park's integration into the urban web of the area. The design of the park, based on a series of paths which assume the shape of a tree's branches, further enhances this integration. The main characteristic of the project is the large lake which stretches across the park and which connects the street to the beach via a walkway above the water. The lake is built on different levels and in varying shapes to enhance the waterfalls and the other aspects of this large expanse of water.

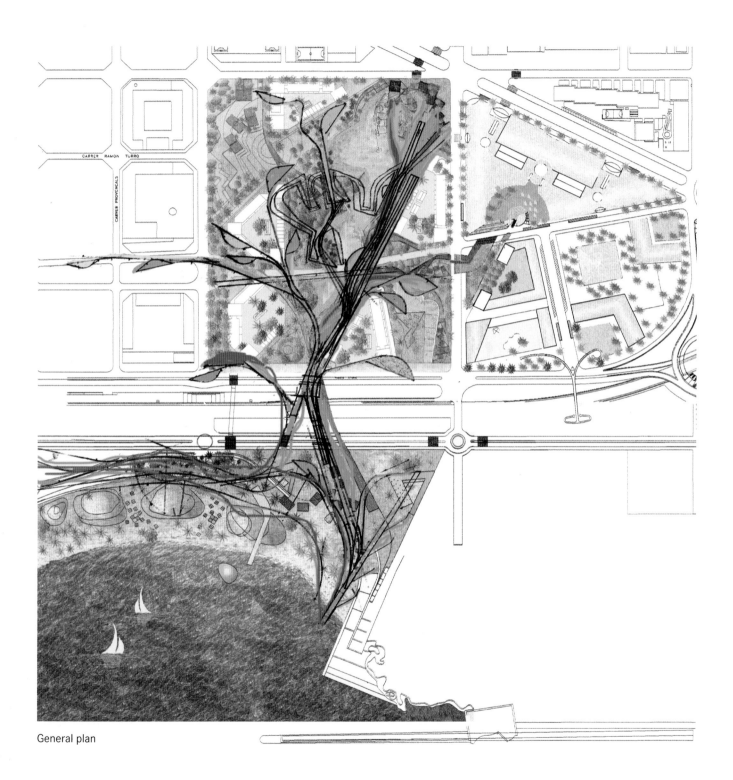

General plan

The presence of water, as
much the sea as the artificial
lake, determines the
vegetation of the park.
Original species of marshes
predominate.

Alexander Kiellands Plass | **Grindaker**

Oslo, Norway, 2001 This park is situated on a slope in a zone of dense urban traffic in the center of Oslo, Norway. The original project was designed in the 1920's but over time it declined into a dark area of little interest. In 1998, because of the celebrations in preparation for the new millennium, the town council decided to renovate various emblematic public spaces, including the Alexander Kiellands Plass. The first stage of the project was the creation of a green open space, bordered by rows of trees situated at the ends of the park. The use of water elements defines the different zones and heightens the beauty of the park for the visitor. The river Ila, which flows 32.8' (10 m) underground, was brought to the surface and redirected through the park using a sequence of wells and fountains which follow the natural slope of the land. Many trees were cut down in order to increase the shape and size of the park and add light.

The water takes on different forms as it flows through the park, from calm reflecting pools to lively and dynamic fountains which decorate some of the open esplanades.

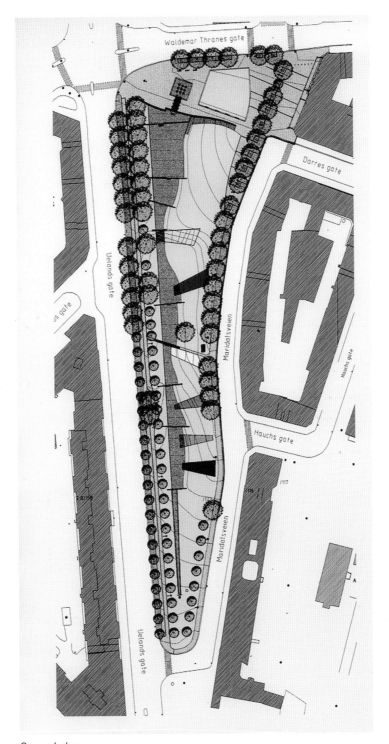

General plan

General Mills Corporation | **oslund.and.assoc.**

Golden Valley, MN, USA, 2004 The campus of the General Mills Corporation was originally designed by Skidmore Owings and Merrill in 1950, using a modern architectonic plan in a wild scenic setting. The acquisition of a new corporation called for the campus to be enlarged to house the new employees. The architectonic style needed to complement the existing building and frame the new open space situated in front. The initial idea was that the new buildings should appear to be floating, just above a still plane of water. The vegetation which is found on both sides of the building strengthens the geometric composition of the space and establishes a link between the buildings and nature. The water reflection, the adjacent platforms, and the gentle grassy hills create the ideal framework in which to position a series of large sculptures throughout the open space.

The water reflection enhances the architectonic shapes of the building, creating a transitory space between the building and nature and helping to separate the different outdoor spaces.

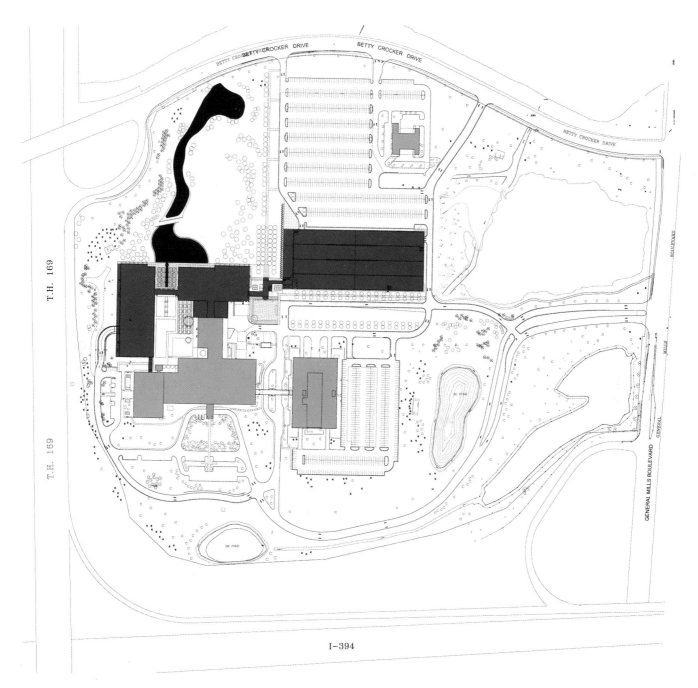

Betty Crocker Drive

Betty Crocker Drive

Betty Crocker Drive

T.H. 169

T.H. 169

General Mills Boulevard

General Mills Boulevard

I-394

General plan

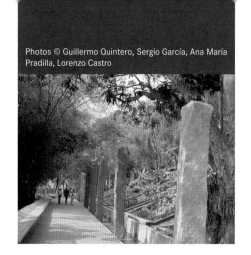

Water Park | **Lorenzo Castro**

Bucaramanga, Colombia, 2003　Since its beginnings in the 1930's, the water treatment plant known as "the Morrorrico tanks" was the center of attraction for the inhabitants of Bucaramanga, in the north of Colombia. In addition to providing drinking water, it was also used as a recreational area for the locals. This use was institutionalized and people were free to use the area for both purposes for many years. About twenty years ago, the company decided to close it to the public. From that day on, the plant became an isolated zone of the town, which deteriorated gradually. The Bucaramanga Metropolitan Aqueduct Company decided to reopen the complex to the public and integrate the area into the urban web by rescuing its history and highlighting the positive aspects of the place. The intervention used a strict orthogonal geometry to complement the existing buildings and soften the lie of the land. The resulting contrast of elements creates a new landscape which enhances the existing one and invites the inhabitants of the town to use the area once more for recreation.

Water determines the
character of the walkways
and the different spaces
within the park in the form of
fountains, waterfalls, jets of
water, trickles, or ponds.

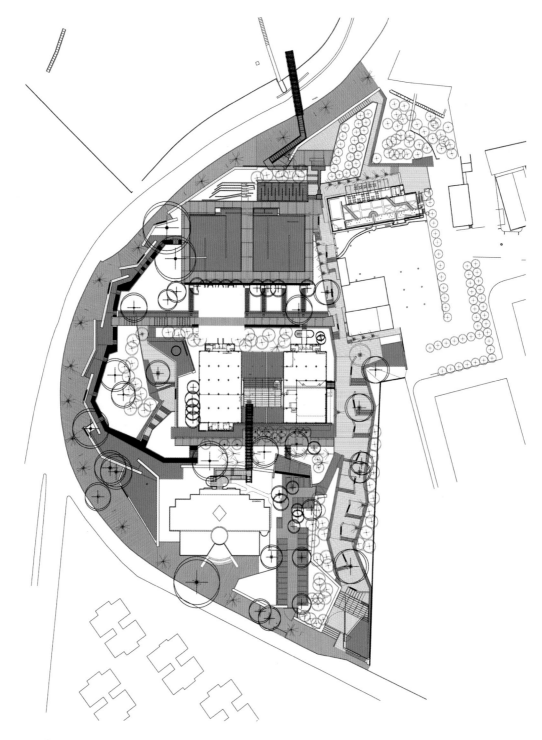

General plan

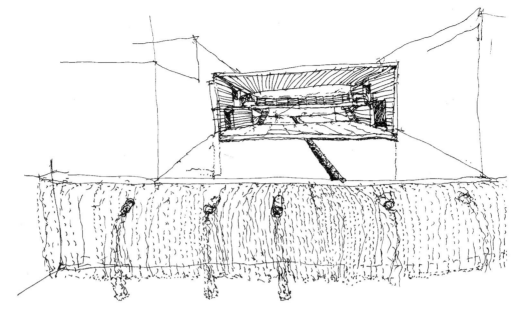

Sketch

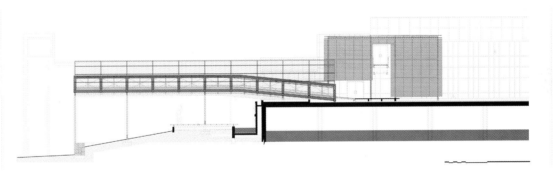

Section

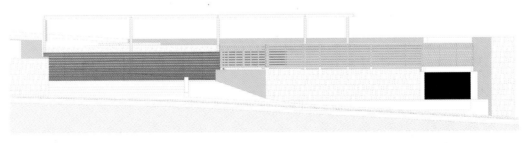

Elevation

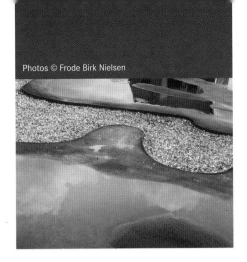

Noerresundby Urban Garden | **SLA**

Aalborg, Denmark, 2005 This project concerns the restoration of a small public garden in Noerresundby in the north of Denmark. The garden has traditionally been frequented by groups of school children who use this quiet corner of the city to share their sensory and creative experiences. The project, a series of organic platforms which sit on top of a graveled area, is envisaged as a place for kids to play and explore. Some of the platforms house masses of vegetation or create shallow ponds that mimic artificial puddles. A series of water fountains come alive seven times a day like artificial geysers, throwing the water up several meters and then storing it in the ponds. The garden is surrounded by a rustic metal fence which delimits the area and creates a direct visual connection with the urban setting.

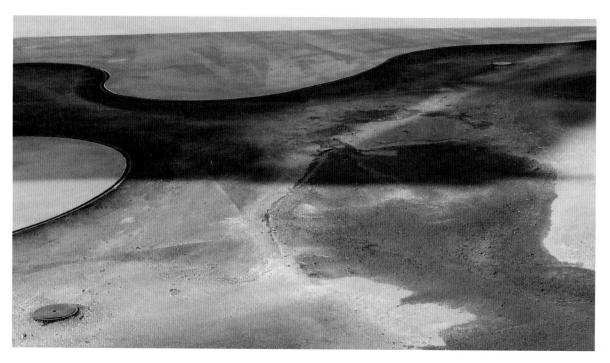

The organic design of the
platforms and the marks left
by the water fountain
throughout the day create a
natural effect, as though the
garden was part of the
surrounding scenery.

NYGADE

MELLEMBROERNE

General plan

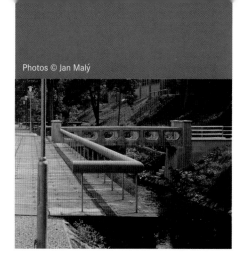

Loučná River Dyke | **Josef Pleskot/AP Atelier**

Litomyšl, Czech Republic, 2002 The town of Litomyšl in the Czech Republic is classified as a world heritage site. It has experienced intense development over recent decades, which has led to the enlargement of the town's urban zones. The modification of the dike in the river Loučná, which was formerly in an out-of-town area, is part of the global strategy to integrate the new urban areas. On the other hand, the project had to include a control system against flooding and create a pleasant public space for a population of about 11,000. The project design established a clear contrast with the modern architectonic setting of the new development using a language inspired by nature. The sizeable stone walls, the wooden platforms, and the organic embankments create a natural image, evoking memories of the region's canals. In this way the dike has been converted into an attractive public space which is connected to the historical center of the town.

The combination of rustic materials, such as stone, brick, and wood, heightens the natural character of the project and its integration with the surroundings.

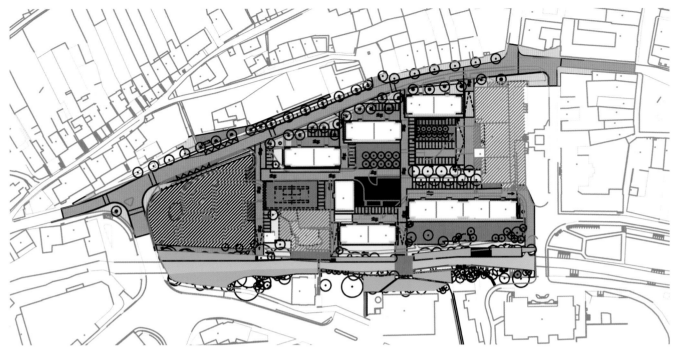

General plan

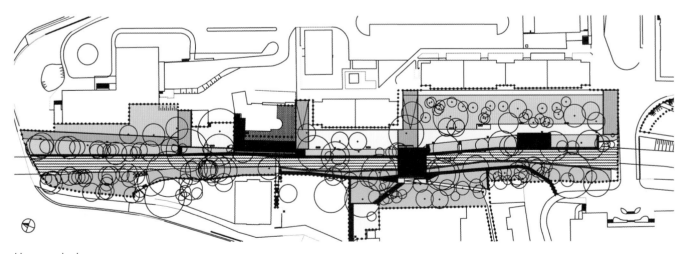

Linear park plan

The project uses different levels of platforms above the riverbed, which in turn give rise to different outlooks over the surroundings.

Bridges

Bridges

Foot Bridge | **Miró Rivera Architects**

Austin, TX, USA The inspiration for this lightweight bridge: The reeds which border the lake where it is located. The foot bridge was also part of a general plan to protect the peninsula's delicate ecosystem. Visitors can find abundant flora and fauna as well as various species of migratory birds which nest in this nature reserve thanks to a network of footpaths. The footpaths and the bridge were both designed with a view to enhance the fragility of the ecosystem and bestow a feeling of respect for the environment. The image of the bridge uses rusty metal rods which serve as the handrails. The structure is made up of two arch-shaped pipes which stretch 78.7' (24 m) over the lake. The effect of the rods intertwining like roots and branches camouflage the bridge in its setting. The end of the lake and the surrounding scenery can be viewed on crossing the bridge.

Two white concrete blocks give support to both sides of the bridge's metal structure and serve as the dividing element between the bridge and the natural setting.

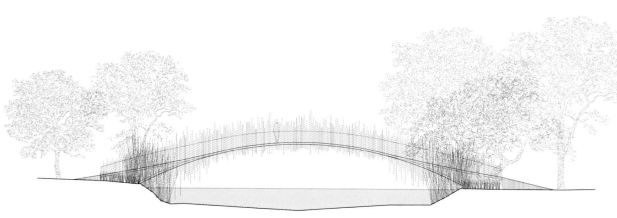

Elevation

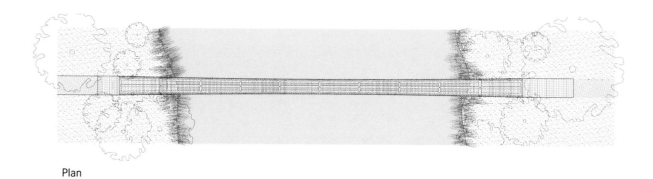

Plan

Hemelwater Bridge | **Wissing**

The Haige, Holland, 2002 The name of this bridge, Hemelwater, means "water from heaven" or "rain." The name refers to the source of the water which passes below. In the past, this area was surrounded by typical Dutch countryside, with wide open fields, small water dikes, and herds of cows and sheep. Due to urban sprawl this district is now part of the suburbs of the Hague and a large canal was needed to provide water to the surrounding neighborhood. Thus, a new bridge had to be built to allow the pedestrians, vehicles, and even the trams to circulate. The original aim was to project the image of a high-quality urban development zone. The three pillars which support the bridge resemble giant gondolas which float just above the water level, thus creating a group of terraces like balcony lookouts, where people can relax and enjoy the panoramic views of the canal and its surroundings.

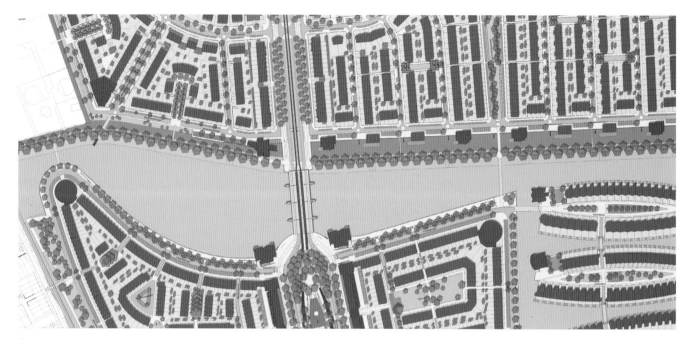

General plan

Models

The bridge serves as a
longitudinal square above the
water. In the summer,
children use the terraces as
play areas and diving
platforms.

Geometric Hot Springs | **Germán del Sol**

Villarica National Park, Chile, 2003 This project involved developing the thermal hot springs which erupt naturally in a nearly inaccessible gorge, at the heart of the lush forests of the Villarrica National Park in Chile. There are over sixty thermal springs which produce more than 5.3 gallons (20 l) of water per second at temperatures of around 176°F (80°C). The project uses wooden walkways which travel along the valley bottom, allowing the visitor to enjoy the bathing facilities. This was achieved by excavating twenty wells along the 1,476' (450 m) ravine in and amongst the exuberant vegetation. The walkways, which are flat surfaces without steps, allow people to explore the ravine with ease in order to find the ideal private spot for bathing, without having to worry about tripping up when it gets dark or sliding on ice in the winter. The project, as well as the walkways, also includes toilets, changing areas, and a series of terraces which provide spots to relax, and enjoy the views of the surrounding forest.

This rustic yet extremely precise architectonic project makes the experience of relaxing in these purifying hot spring waters accessible to everyone.

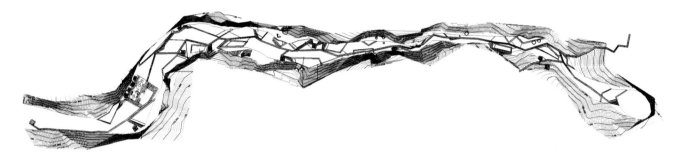

General plan

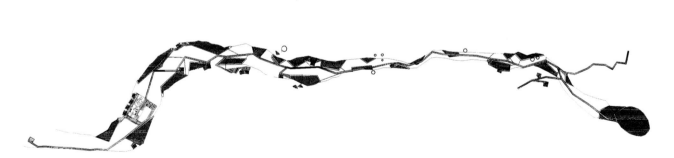

Path plan

Squares

Squares

Pedestrian Zone of Innichen | **Alles Wird Gut**

Innichen, Austria, 2002 Innichen is a small village located in the Dolomites mountain range, on the border between Austria and Italy, whose urban development is marked by its location between two routes. Today, the intersection of these routes is still maintained as the central public space of the village. Over time, it has become the social and economic center of the valley where the main public infrastructures converge. In recent years there has also been a surge in tourism. Due to this, and like so many other tourist centers, the community decided to reduce the traffic in the historic center and transform the streets and squares, formerly open to vehicles, into pedestrian areas. Using a contemporary and innovative design, the original character of the village's public spaces have been restored. The lie of the land and the architecture which defines the open space is a determining factor in the new design.

A series of platforms with different characters and atmospheres create zones of intense activity or extreme peace, as is the case of the pond shown here.

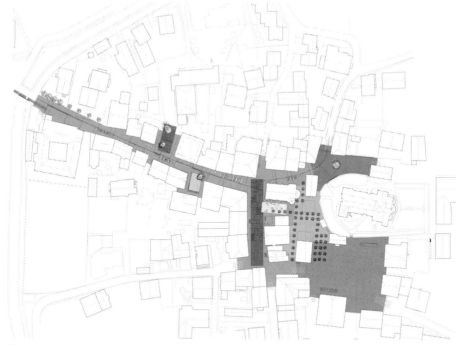

General plan

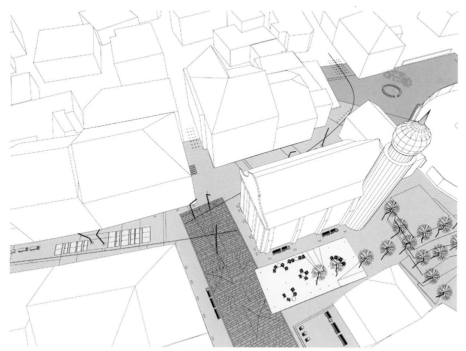

Perspective

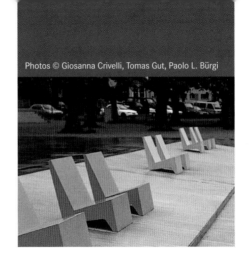

Pier Square | **Paolo L. Bürgi**

Kreuzlingen, Switzerland, 2003 The town of Kreuzlingen, in the northeast region of Switzerland, maintains a close relationship with the lake of the same name and on whose shore the town has grown. However, the water-front has developed haphazardly and little care has been taken to establish a clear relationship between the town and the lake. The project for this square creates a new link from the town to the lake and from the lake to the town. The basic idea was to allow access from both directions in order to establish a new entrance way to the town. The sizeable concrete square stretches horizontally from the old pier and its natural slope submerges gently into the waters of the lake. The platform, with a couple of steps, incorporates a series of painted concrete benches on which to sit and enjoy the view. A fountain, also built in concrete, resembles a canal which has eroded the rocky surface on which it is placed.

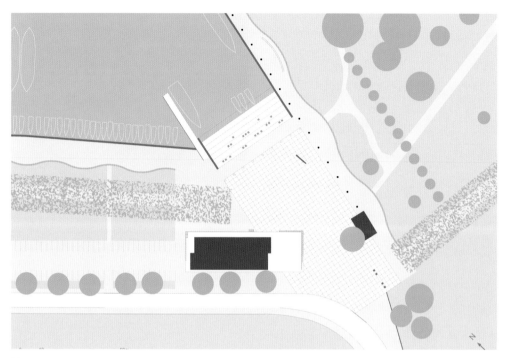

Plan

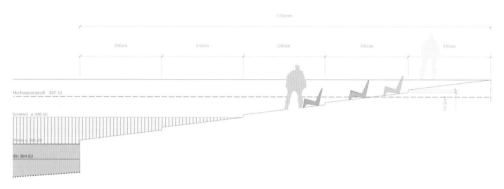

Section

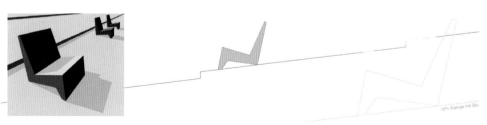

Details

Aguas Square | **Dal Pian Arquitectos Associados**

Campinas, Brazil, 2004   At the end of 2003, the local water company in Campinas, Brazil, decided to organize a public competition for the architectonic re-assessment of the town's principal drinking water reserve. The precinct is found close to the old city center, an aging and deteriorating architectonic complex which dates back to the end of the nineteenth century. The project, which concerned the design of the public space in the square, also involved the renovation of local services, such as a cultural center, a cinema, and a medical center. The winning idea establishes a series of varied spaces for the public areas which are part of the old precinct's esplanade. The design envisages four rows of urban elements, each with independent functions as well as working together in order to strengthen the public character of the square. These four rows are made up of a strip of trees, creating a shady area; stone benches sheltered from the sun; a row of fountains; and a water feature which stretches lengthways at one end of the square.

This project, as well as restoring the old precinct of the town's water company, has also served as a springboard for the urban renovation of the center of Campinas.

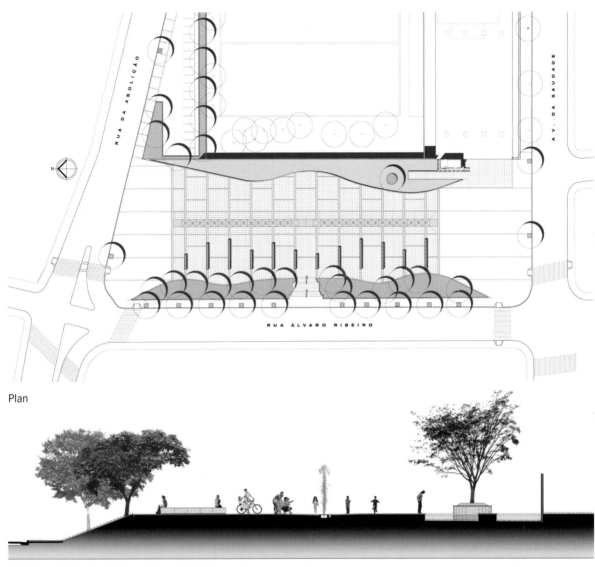

Plan

Section

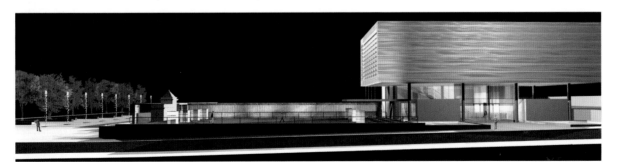

Rendering

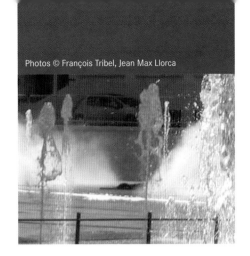

François Mitterrand Square | **JML Arquitectura del Agua**

Creusot, France, 2005 In 2004, the Heart of the Town urban design project was launched in order to restore the central zone of the French town of Creusot. The project is characterized by the strong presence of water which is used in different ways along the route, starting in the town hall and culminating in François Mitterrand Square. The design of this square, an integral part of the urban setting, aims to extol the qualities of water so that it can be seen and heard from anywhere on the esplanade. The project solves the problem of traffic by subtly integrating it in the design of the square. Different types of granite paving stones have been cleverly laid out to separate the use of each zone of the square, in this way differentiating the vehicle zone from the pedestrian zone. The water fountains help to fashion the various spaces within the square and create a sense of peace and freshness in the hottest months of the year.

The diverse architectonic
forms surrounding the square
merge together via a
monolithic granite carpet. The
carpet also serves as a
defining feature.

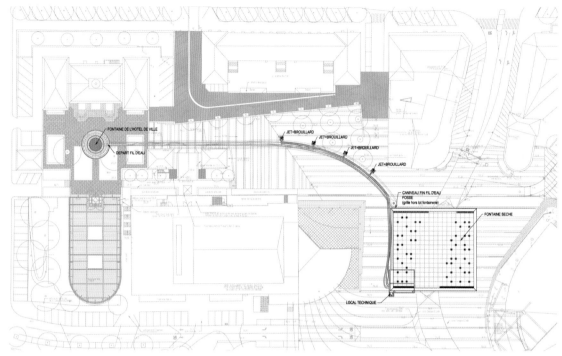

General plan

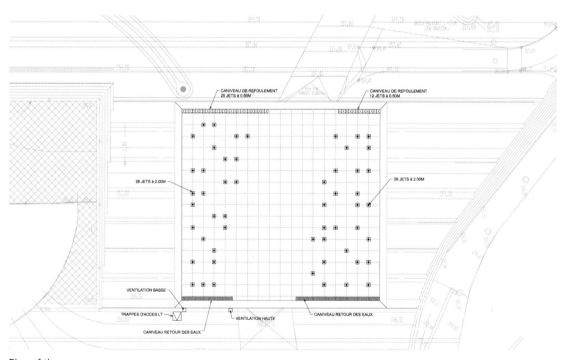

Plan of the square

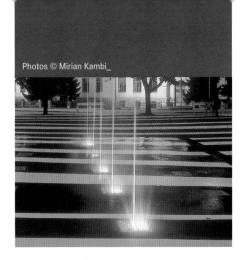

Čufarjev Square | **Scapelab**

Jesenice, Slovenia, 2003 The restoration of Čufarjev Square began with the idea of creating a small public space. This, in turn, generated a transformation of the environment over the years. In spite of the square's small size, large-scale commitments are involved in the project with regard to the existing architecture, the urban link, the surrounding scenery, and the economic and social factors. The square, surrounded by public buildings such as a school, a bookshop, a theatre, a cinema, and a bar, needed to be an open space which linked the different activities. The design of the square, selected from a public competition, complies with the town's petition to create a traditional square with a fountain. The new square is conceived as a flat, multi-use surface in which a single fountain was placed free from any other traditional objects which could block the visibility of the whole. The materials used help project an austere and modest image, as though it were a work of infrastructure.

The fountain is built into the
surface of the square itself,
which means it can be used
for large public events such
as concerts, parties, or public
meetings.

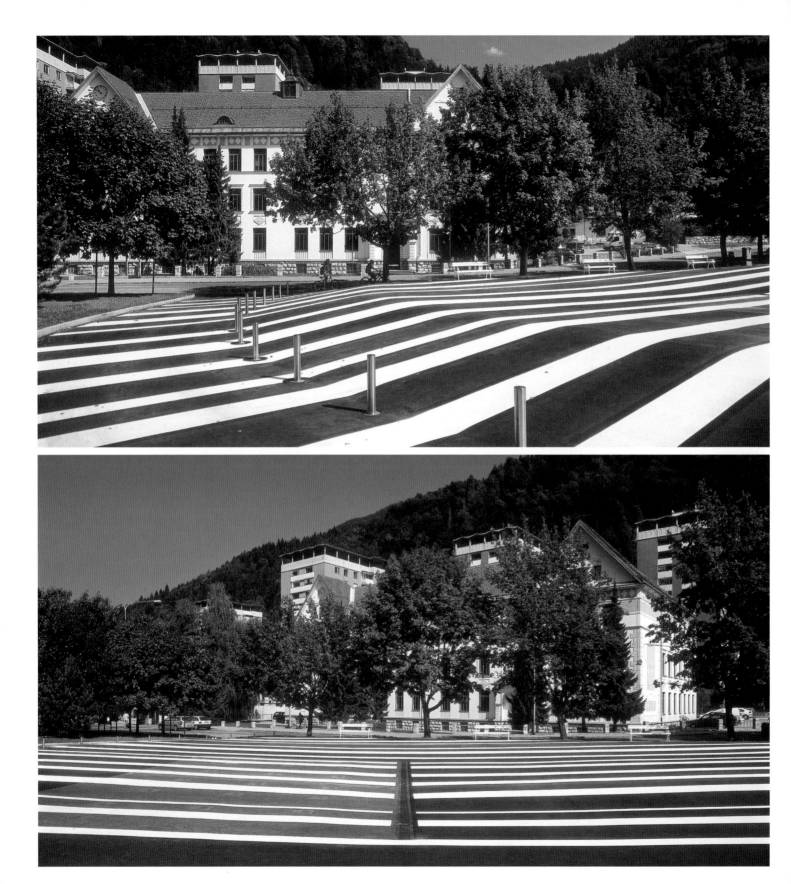

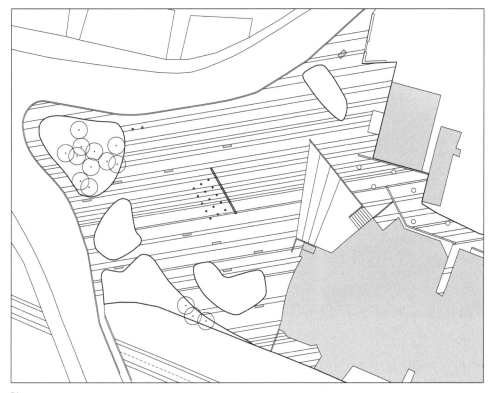

Plan

The changes in color at the
edges of the square give a
dynamic energy to the project
and promote the participation
of the townsfolk.

Photos © Stéphane Llorca

Nombre d'Or Square | **JML Arquitectura del Agua**

Montpellier, France, 2001

Nombre D'Or Square was designed in 1980 by the Spanish architect Ricardo Bofill in the town of Montpellier, France. The original objective was to promote a new zone of the town uniting shops, offices, and dwellings. Nearly two decades later the town hall organized a competition to redevelop the square, including an ornamental fountain. The winning solution consisted of a pyramid composition which achieves the various functional and formal aspects of the project. On the one hand, it refers to the name of the square, given that gold is numerically represented by a triangle. On the other hand, it maintains the visual connection with the commercial axis which crosses the neighborhood. The fountain is truly dynamic and can alternate between water shooting up and water pyramids. At 9 p.m. the highest water jet tells the time and continues rising and falling. Over time the fountain has become an icon of this area of the town and an integral part of the architectonic framework of the zone.

The different shapes of water
create a picture of movement,
transforming the square
throughout the day.

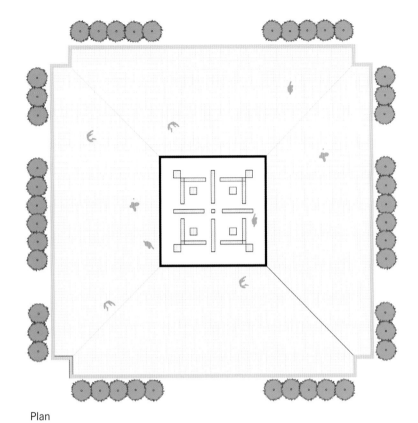

Plan

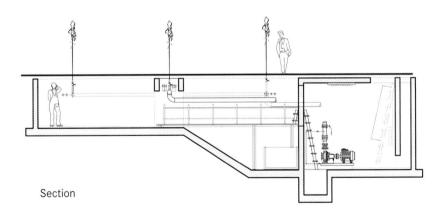

Section

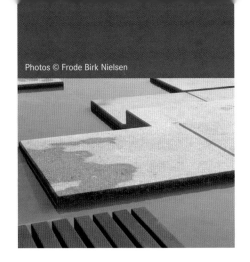

Harbour Square | **Birk Nielsen Tegnestue**

Thisted, Denmark, 2005 Thisted, a small town in the north of Denmark, is an interesting destination for Danes and foreigners alike thanks to its long tradition as commercial enclave of the North Sea. In order to promote the culture of the town and to create a suitable urban infrastructure for tourism, the town hall created Bedre Byrum, a development plan for the town's urban areas. Part of this plan concerns the restoration of the most important historic sites and thoroughfares, such as the Harbour Square. This emblematic public space is the culmination of Storegade, an important road in the historic center, and the main pier for the boats which weigh anchor around the bay. The project aims to restore this nerve center of the town and to pay tribute to the close relationship the town has always maintained with the sea. The square is designed to unite leisure areas and interactive areas; for example, holding small concerts around a composition of concrete blocks on top of a pool of water, as though the bay itself is flowing into town.

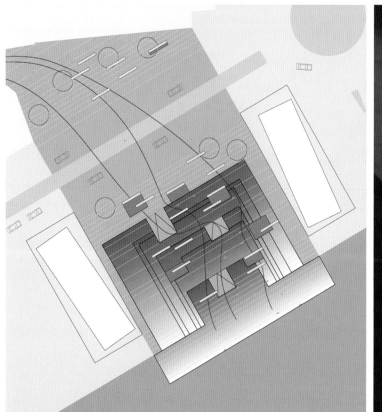
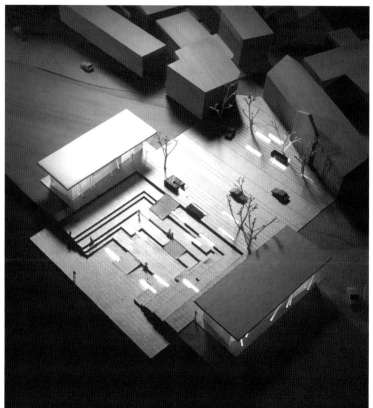

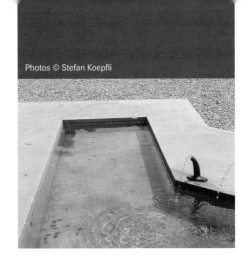

St. Karl's Public School | **Koepfli Partner**

Altdorf, Switzerland, 2002   The design of this public school's patio in Altdorf, Switzerland is an exercise in reducing the space in which the main functional elements required in this type of recreational area have been enhanced. The project consists of an open area, covered in fine gravel, which gives great flexibility. It can serve as an area for running, a games area, or a place for outdoor meetings, etc. Several trees, mostly situated on the perimeter, create a varied landscape, providing shade, while the large concrete benches at the outer limits of the patio are used for rest areas or to observe the surrounding activity. The central point of this simple composition and main attraction for the kids is the fountain, which takes pride of place in the center of the space. Its unique geometry, which mimics the actual geometry of the area of the school, makes this a reference point, as though it was a monolithic sculpture which bestows character on the place. The polished concrete, its monolithic look, and the gray color which blends with the gravel on the ground highlights the somber character of the space.

Plan

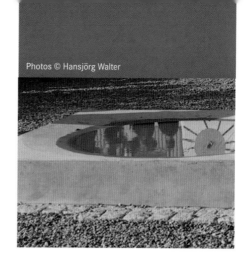

Pausenplatz | **Team Landschaftsarchitekten**

Hallau, Switzerland, 2002 This garden, which runs along a gentle south-facing hillside and across a neighboring vineyard, is the central point of a primary school in Hallau, Switzerland. The design of this recreational and meeting area seeks to optimize the panoramic views from throughout the garden. The project started with a small artificial stream whose source is at the high point of the playground and which flows down the natural slope of the land, finishing in a tree-filled courtyard in the bottom part of the school. All along this defining feature are different playgrounds, situated on different levels, with amazing views over the vineyards. The fences and low walls, which serve as benches, border each area and enhance the topography of the land. Two water fountains mark the start and end of the small stream which the kids use to play in or to drink. Thanks to a simple design, this project has created an array of spaces with unique character offering diverse possibilities.

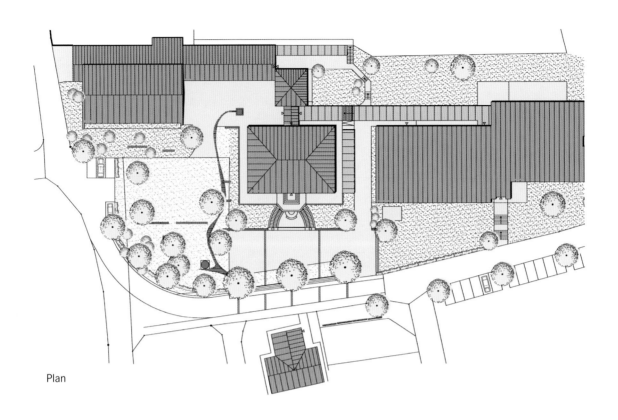

Plan

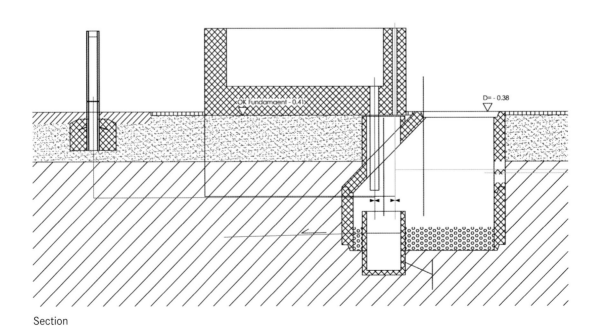

Section

130

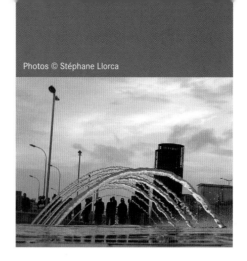

Barcelona Trade Fair | **JML Arquitectura del Agua**

Barcelona, Spain, 2005 In recent years Barcelona's trade fair zone has undergone many transformations, including the construction of a new complex of pavilions designed by the Japanese architect Toyo Ito. The complex is situated in a former suburban zone, which today is part of the metropolitan network. It was envisaged as an urban gateway to the town. This is partly the result of its location, at the center of important access routes to the city, and partly due to the very character of the trade fair program. The exterior zones are made up of large access halls to the pavilions, designed like small, curving interconnected squares. A number of fountains sit on the edges in order to separate the pedestrian area from the road. The design of the fountains is in keeping with the ideas of the Japanese architect and consists of numerous jets of water which create smooth curves, emphasizing the very geometry of the complex.

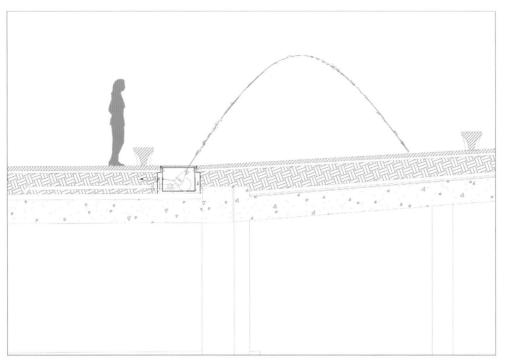

Section

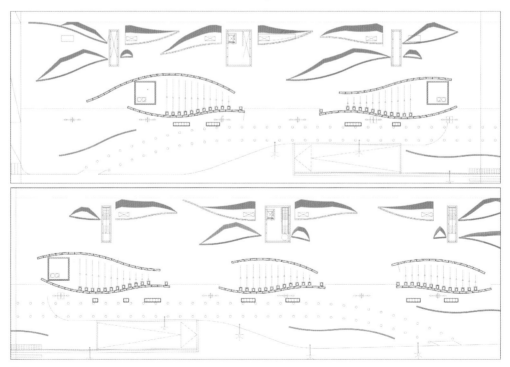

Plans

Borders

Borders

Pedestrian Walkway of Deer Moat | **Josef Pleskot/AP Atelier**

Prague, Czech Republic 2002 The pedestrian walkway of Deer Moat began with the initiative started by the president of the Czech Republic himself. His goal: to create an alternative pedestrian access from the river Vltava to Prague castle. The new route facilitates the access to the castle for visitors from the center of town, giving the public the chance to enjoy this truly rich scenic environment. The design of the walkway maintains, for the majority of its length, the same route as the stream which flows along the mountain, and the dam which has been used as the main component of the project. This prevents any blockage of the flow of water and converts it into the connecting theme of the walkway. The most surprising element of the alteration is the oval-shaped tunnel, which goes through the mountain and allows the path and riverbed to be followed more directly. The 255.9' (78 m) of brick-covered tunnel and the sound of the water which runs under the metal netting path recall the internal structure of the castle.

The oval shape and the brick covering are changed at both ends of the tunnel and are made into large rectangular doors of reinforced concrete.

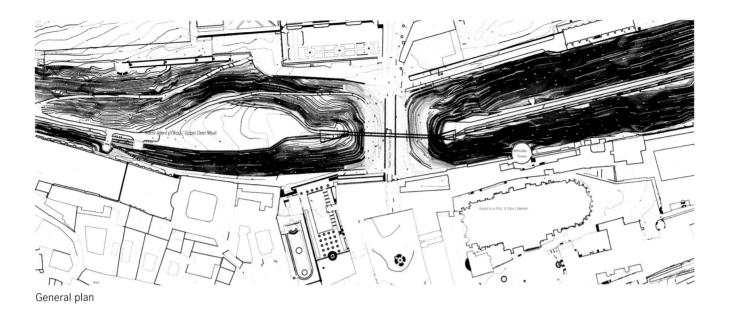

General plan

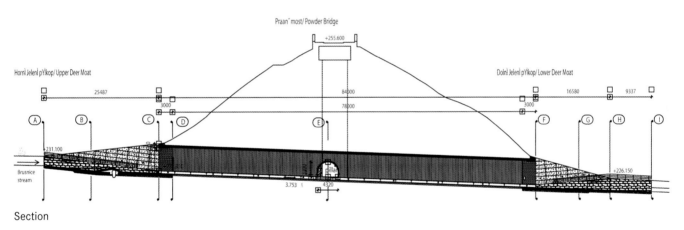

Praan˘ most/ Powder Bridge

+255.600

Horní Jelení pŸíkop/ Upper Deer Moat

Dolní Jelení pŸíkop/ Lower Deer Moat

25487

3000

84000

78000

16580

9337

3000

(A) (B) (C) (D) (E) (F) (G) (H) (I)

231.100

+226.150

Brusnice
stream

3.753

4320

Section

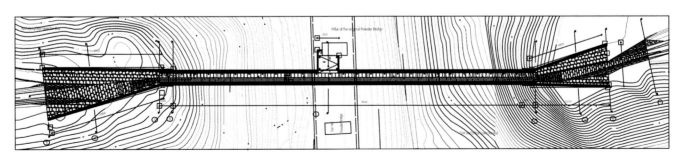

Pillar of the original Powder Bridge

Tunnel plan

143

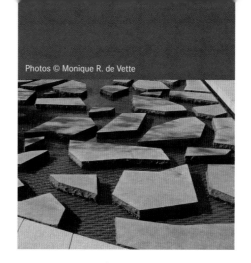

Roombeek | **Buro Sant En Co**

Enschede, Holland, 2005 In May 2000 a fireworks factory exploded in Enschede, Holland and destroyed a number of nearby houses. The damaged district began an urban reconstruction which was carried out in close collaboration with the residents. The main objective was to create an attractive plan and provide the necessary public infrastructure for the old and new inhabitants. The plan was to design small neighborhoods, each with its own identity, which were linked by a system of long strips of land which follow the original outline of the neighborhood. Roombeek is a commercial street and also the main urban core of the district. The small stream, which gives name to the street and had in the past flowed underground, has been restored and brought up to the surface once again. Now the water is part of the urban environment and has become the district's new central point. Its asymmetrical design, which widens and narrows along the street, accentuates its different spatial features.

The stream flows along under an original composition of stones which also serve as stepping stones, taking inspiration from nature's hazardous character.

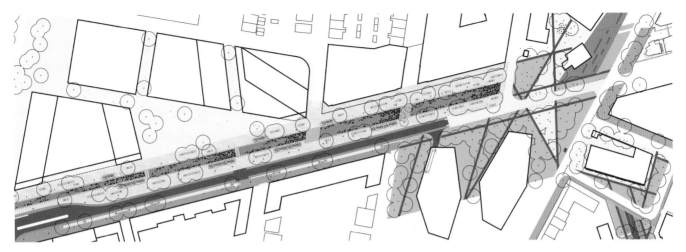

General plan

Section

| 8.60 meter trottoir | 7.20 meter beek (variabel) | 4.50 meter trottoir | parkeerpl. 2.30 m. | 1.50 m. fietspad | 4.50 meter rijweg | 1.50 m. fietspad | parkeerpl. 2.00 m. | trottoir 4.20m |

Exploded view

Central Water Park | **Sasaki Associates**

Indianapolis, IN, USA, 2000 The urban design project for the banks of the White river, which flows through Indianapolis, began with the creation of a system of open spaces which serve as a unifying element in this zone of the city. The project aims to establish new links between the center of the town and the river zone which had, until now, been ignored as part of the public space. The goal: to transform the river banks into an area of scenic beauty suitable for recreational activities and which meet the demands of the community. The master plan was to be developed over the 9.3 miles (15 km) of land created by the flow of the river through the city. A series of smaller passages connect this new lineal park with other symbolic public spaces in the urban center. Other parks and larger spaces near the riverside have also been renovated and serve as urban settings for the metropolitan area, making the river a linking element within the town.

The project incorporates
elements which recall the
former uses of the area over
the past 200 years, such
as the canals and industrial
structures.

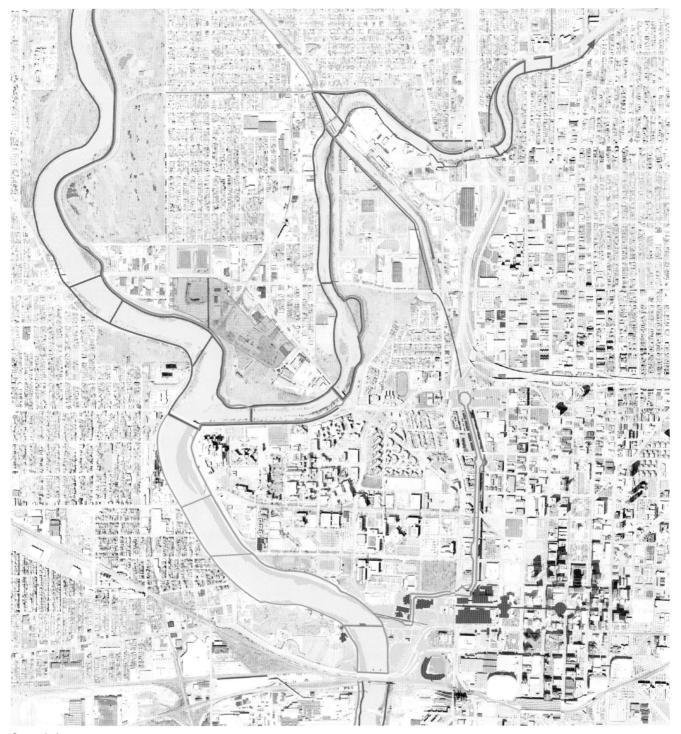

General plan

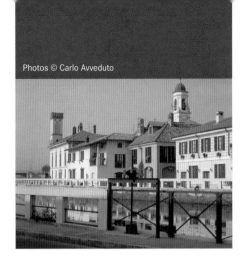

Public Space in Gaggiano | **Luigi Ferrario**

Gaggiano, Italy, 2003 The town of Gaggiano, about 18.6 miles (30 km) west of Milan, is a small island on the Naviglio Grande, one of the canals built in the Middle Ages. The canals were designed to open up Milan to the sea; this converted it into the main fluvial port of Italy at the end of the 19th century. The close relationship the town has with water due to its unique geographical situation has made the public space of Gaggiano a true balcony overlooking the canal. Over time this has deteriorated due to the invasion of vehicles. This restructuring of the town's waterfront heightens its original qualities, restores the two shorelines as pedestrian zones, and eases the navigation in this stretch of the canal. The design is somber and uses traditional regional materials as well as the latest illumination and water vaporization technology. Along with limestone, paving stones, and metal, water is the fourth material which completes the project. The area is defined by the fountains and water springs situated at ground level and bordered by stone elements.

The urban "furniture," such as benches, handrails, waste bins, and tree wells, are made from double steel, which creates an airy feel.

General plan

Riverside plan

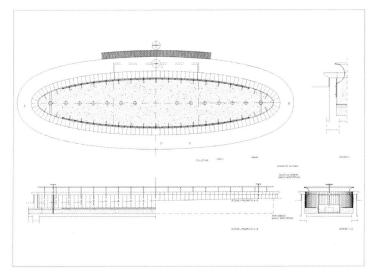

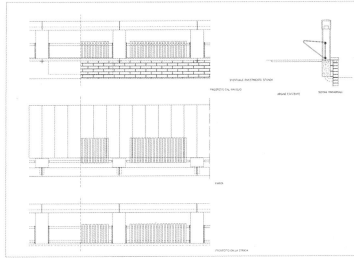

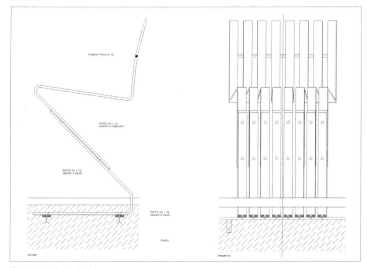

Construction details

Oriental Bay | **Isthmus Group, Architecture Workshop**

Wellington, New Zealand, 2003   Oriental Bay is considered by the community of Wellington, New Zealand, to be the jewel in the city's crown. The bay contains a series of small beaches and quays of great scenic beauty and evokes the very history of the town's founding. In order to redesign this waterfront, the designers worked closely with engineers and other specialists to identify and understand the changes which the coast in this zone has undergone. The project needed to boost the recreational activities as well as conserve the historic character of the waterfront. An artificial reef had to be built in order to protect the coast from the open sea and keep the sand in place. This has resulted in the creation of a sea wall, made up of a series of platforms, using a three-dimensional network. This protects the beach and provides a new public space.

The three-level platform
system is designed for public
use, and also protects the bay
from the lashing tides.

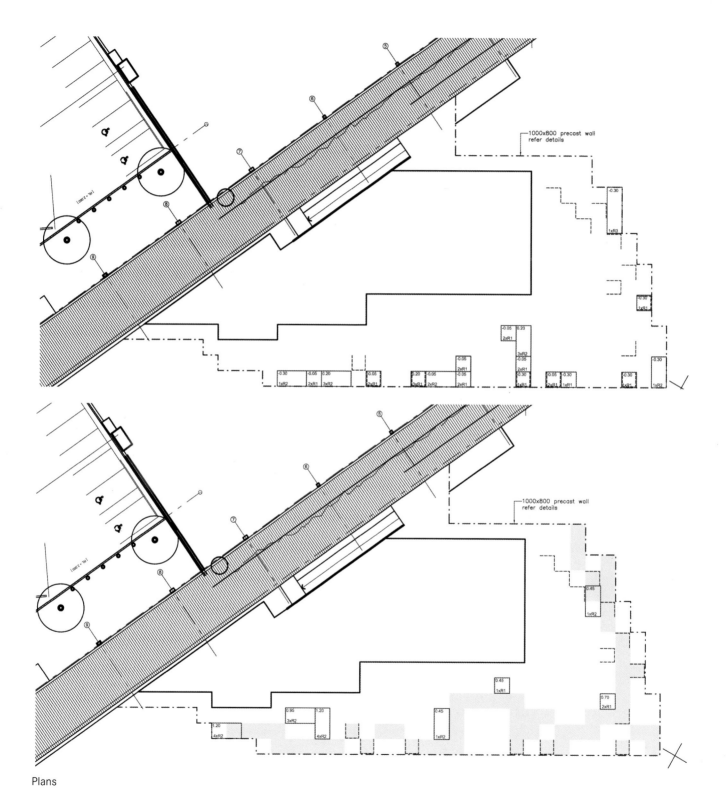

Plans

This development creates a
series of public spaces, such
as the quay, a grassy
esplanade, a gazebo, and the
beach, which allows for
different settings and uses of
the waterfront.

Photos © Stefan Koepfli

Seebad Zweiern | **Koepfli Partner**

Rotkreuz, Switzerland, 2004   This former bathing area on the Zug Lake, in the central region of Switzerland, was traditionally used by the locals. In accordance with the regulations for this type of spa, the area had to be redesigned and made suitable for its safe and correct use. The first phase involved knocking down part of the perimeter wall which bordered the lake, obstructing the access from the water to the shore. A slightly sloped graveled area has been built in its place, which separates the shore from the grass. Other stretches of the wall have been covered with wood and some contain sand banks for lakeside relaxation. Several wooden platforms, traditionally used in the area, were placed a few meters away from the shore to complete the project. The main objective was to preserve the natural and peaceful character of the place as much as possible and to enhance the surrounding scenery in a discreet manner.

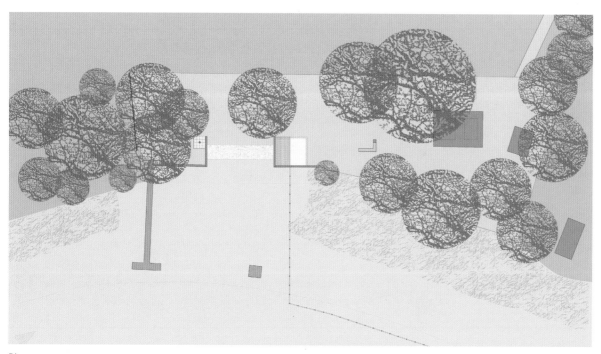

Plan

Respect for the environment is reflected in the delicacy and lightness of each element, thanks to the use of natural materials such as wood and gravel.

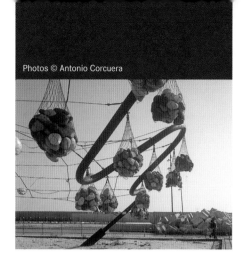

Photos © Antonio Corcuera

Forum 2004 Bathing Area | **Beth Galí, Jaume Benavent/BB+GG Arquitectes**

Barcelona, Spain, 2004 The bathing area is on the seafront which borders the esplanade designed to house the Forum 2004 in Barcelona. Today it is used to hold diverse cultural events for the metropolitan area. The project is presented as an alternative to the bathing areas available along the town's beaches. This difference is reflected in the possibility of enjoying a controlled sea, calm water, and, in the future, thalassotherapy. The design involves the construction of reefs on the coastline to protect the area from the east coast winds and to achieve an ideal area for water sports and other leisure activities. The formal composition of the project is based on the close relationship the area maintains with the surrounding public space, such as the esplanade of the Forum, a park, and a marina. The coast is turned into a stone mooring quay situated 4.9' (1.5 m) above sea level. From here, the quay enters the water via a step ladder which goes more than 3.3' (1 m) under the water. A row of columns emerging from the sea frames the horizon and separates the zones of safe bathing from the open sea.

A series of specially prefabricated pieces of concrete create an architectonic base which adapts to various features, such as sun loungers, ramps, tables, or showers.

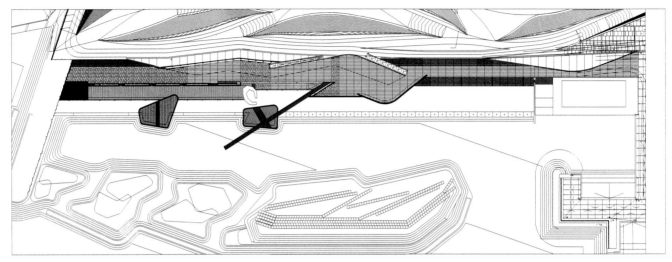

Plan

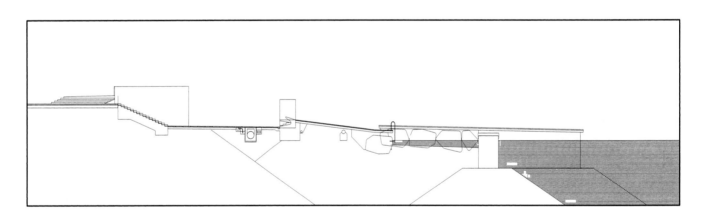

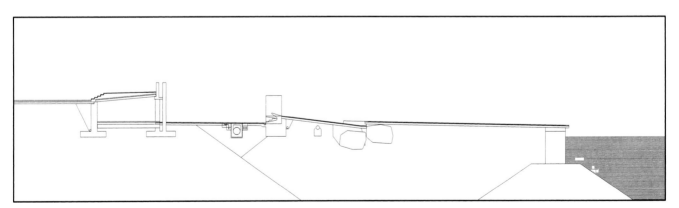

Sections

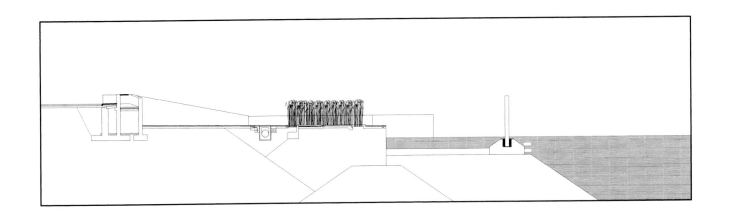

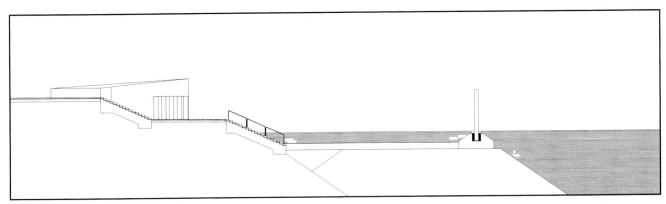

Sections

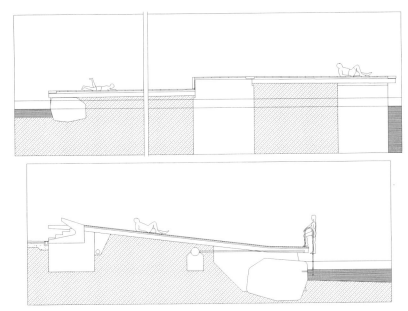

Sections

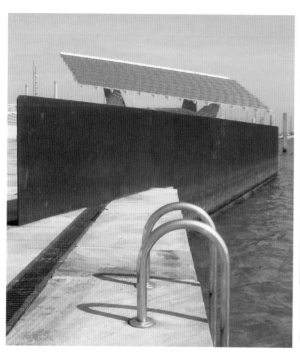

The two marble-covered platforms, which resemble small islands of ice floating in the sea, make the perfect spot for diving into the water.

Cendon di Silea | **Made Associati**

Cendon di Silea, Italy, 2004 This project is the result of a public competition set up by the local council of Silea in Treviso, Italy, to revalue the fluvial environment of the town's urban core. The original idea was to create an architectonic project which bestowed character on the place, highlighted the historic and scenic elements of the area, and heightened public interest. The design took the traditionally characteristic elements of the zone, such as rows of fences or types of vegetation, to create a system of small-scale urban stages which connect the river shore with the public space of the town. The various resting places generated throughout the composition allow the visitor different viewpoints. The project also restores the shoreline as a pier for small boats, which enabled the creation of a series of platforms. These are located about 23" (60 cm) above the level of the pier and are converted into panoramic balconies overlooking the river.

The rustic finishes of the
materials used in the project,
like steel, wood, and stone,
help integrate the composition
into the natural setting.

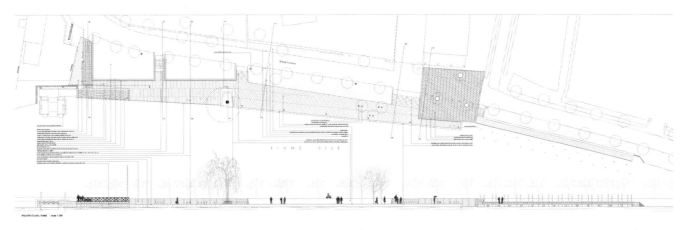

General plan and section

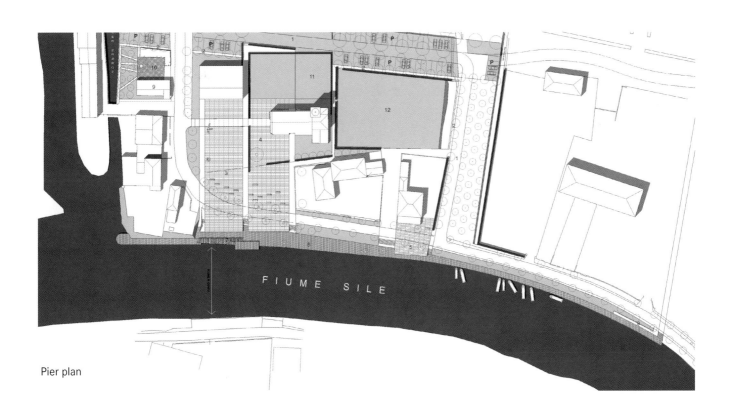

Pier plan